FROM STARTUP TO STARDOM

Unlocking the Secrets to Business Triumph and Public Adoration.

By

Mary J. Ballard

COPYRIGHT

Copyright © 2024 Mary J. Ballard

All rights reserved. No part of this publication may be reproduced, distributed, or transmitted in any form or by any means, including photocopying, recording, or other electronic or mechanical methods, without the prior written permission of the publisher, except in the case of brief quotations embodied in critical reviews and certain other noncommercial uses permitted by copyright law.

DISCLAIMER

The information provided in this book is for educational and informational purposes only. It is not intended to be a substitute for professional advice, diagnosis, or treatment. Always seek the advice of your physician, financial advisor, or other qualified professional with any questions you may have regarding a medical condition, financial situation, or other matters.

The author and publisher of this book have made every effort to ensure that the information presented is accurate and up to date at the time of publication. However, they make no representations or warranties of any kind, express or implied, about the completeness, accuracy, reliability, suitability, or availability of the information contained herein.

Any reliance you place on such information is strictly at your own risk. The author and publisher will not be liable for any loss or damage arising from your use of this book, including but not limited to direct, indirect, incidental, punitive, and consequential damages.

The inclusion of any links, resources, or references in this book does not imply endorsement or recommendation by the author or publisher. The author and publisher do not endorse, approve, or certify the accuracy, completeness, or usefulness of any information, products, services, or opinions provided by third parties.

ABOUT THE AUTHOR

Mary J. Ballard is an accomplished entrepreneur, business strategist, and author dedicated to helping individuals turn their entrepreneurial dreams into reality. With a passion for innovation and a drive for success, Mary has established herself as a leading voice in the world of entrepreneurship.

Drawing from over a decade of experience in the startup ecosystem, Mary has honed her skills in business development, marketing strategy, and leadership. She has successfully launched and scaled multiple ventures across various industries, from technology startups to sustainable fashion brands.

Mary's entrepreneurial journey began with a vision to create meaningful change in the world. Armed with a Bachelor's degree in Business Administration and fueled by her ambition, she set out to build businesses that not only generate profit but also make a positive impact on society and the environment.

Throughout her career, Mary has been passionate about mentoring aspiring entrepreneurs and sharing her knowledge and insights with others.

She believes in the power of entrepreneurship to drive innovation, create opportunities, and transform lives, and she is committed to helping others unlock their full potential as business leaders.

From Startup to Stardom" is Mary's debut book, born out of her desire to inspire and empower entrepreneurs to achieve success on their own terms. In this book, Mary shares her experiences, strategies, and practical advice to guide readers on their entrepreneurial journey, from launching a startup to reaching new heights of success.

When she's not busy building businesses or writing, Mary enjoys spending time in nature, practicing yoga, and exploring new cultures and cuisines. She is also a passionate advocate for environmental sustainability and social justice, and she strives to incorporate these values into everything she does.

CONTENT

INTRODUCTION... 15

CHAPTER 1:DREAMING BIG................... 27

CHAPTER 2:LAYING THE FOUNDATION... 41

CHAPTER 3: NAVIGATING CHALLENGES... 59

CHAPTER 4:THE ART OF LEADERSHIP... 78

CHAPTER 5: INNOVATION AND ADAPTATION... 92

CHAPTER 6:MARKETING MASTERY.. 106

CHAPTER 7:SCALING HEIGHTS........... 123

CHAPTER 8: FINANCIAL FITNESS....... 141

CHAPTER 9:CULTIVATING SUCCESS.. 158

CHAPTER 10: MAKING AN IMPACT.... 176

CONCLUSION.. 187

INTRODUCTION

Picture this: You're sitting in a cramped apartment, surrounded by stacks of papers and empty coffee cups. Your laptop is open, its screen illuminated by the dim glow of the streetlamp outside. It's late at night, and you're pouring over your business plan for the hundredth time, trying to find the missing piece that will turn your dreams into reality.

This scene may sound familiar to many aspiring entrepreneurs – the late nights, the endless hustle, the unwavering determination to build something from nothing. It's a journey filled with highs and lows, victories and setbacks, but above all, it's a journey of transformation – from startup to stardom.

Welcome to "From Startup to Stardom," where we embark on a thrilling adventure through the world of entrepreneurship, uncovering the secrets to success and unlocking the potential within each of us to achieve greatness.

In this book, we'll explore every aspect of the entrepreneurial journey, from laying the foundation and dreaming big to navigating challenges, mastering marketing, and scaling heights. We'll delve into the art of leadership, innovation, and adaptation, and uncover the keys to financial fitness, cultivating success, and making an impact that extends far beyond the bottom line.

But before we dive into the practical strategies and tactics, let's take a moment to reflect on what it means to be an entrepreneur – to dare to dream, to defy the odds, and to carve out a path of your own in a world filled with uncertainty and opportunity.

For many of us, the journey begins with a spark of inspiration – a bold idea, a passionate vision, or a burning desire to make a difference in the world. It's a moment of clarity, of purpose, of realizing that the status quo is no longer enough, and that we have the power to shape our own destiny.

But inspiration alone is not enough to sustain us on this journey. We must also possess the courage to take action – to step out of our comfort zones, to embrace uncertainty, and to persevere in the face of doubt and adversity.

And so, armed with nothing but a dream and a determination to succeed, we set out on our entrepreneurial journey, navigating the twists and turns of the road ahead with grit, resilience, and a willingness to learn and grow.

Along the way, we encounter challenges – obstacles that threaten to derail us from our path and test our resolve. It may be a lack of funding, a failed product launch, or a setback that forces us to reassess our strategy and adapt to changing circumstances.

But in the face of adversity, we rise to the occasion, drawing strength from within and tapping into our creativity, resourcefulness, and resilience to overcome obstacles and forge ahead towards our goals.

And as we journey further along the road to stardom, we begin to realize that success is not just about achieving our own ambitions, but about making a meaningful impact on the world around us. It's about using our talents, our resources, and our influence to create positive change, to empower others, and to leave a lasting legacy that extends far beyond our own lifetime.

In "From Startup to Stardom," we'll discover the power of entrepreneurship to transform lives, communities, and even entire industries. We'll meet trailblazing entrepreneurs who have defied the odds and achieved remarkable success, and uncover the strategies, mindsets, and habits that have propelled them to greatness

But more than just a roadmap to success, this book is a call to action – a call to dare to dream, to embrace uncertainty, and to seize the opportunities that lie before us. It's a reminder that no matter where we come from or what obstacles we face, we all have the power to create our own destiny and make a meaningful impact on the world.

So join me on this exhilarating journey from startup to stardom, where we'll unlock the secrets to entrepreneurial success and embark on a quest to achieve greatness. Together, we'll defy expectations, defy the odds, and defy gravity itself as we reach for the stars and make our mark on the world.

CHAPTER 1:DREAMING BIG

Dreaming Big" is the spark that ignites the entrepreneurial trip, the motivational force that drives people to achieve their most ambitious pretensions. It's the act of visioning a future that exceeds the limitations of the being situation, daring to imagine what could be rather than what is. At its core, featuring large is about embracing latent creativity and the power of imagination in order to transcend hurdles and revitalize what is possible.

For entrepreneurs, featuring large is a strategic necessity rather than a frivolous pleasure. It acts as the foundation for successful businesses, furnishing the vision and relief necessary to overcome the obstacles and enterprises that come with being an entrepreneur. Featuring large requires creating lofty pretensions that inspire and excite, rallying stakeholders around an analogous vision, and breeding the commitment and fortitude needed to make dreams a reality.

At the heart of big thinking is the belief that one's ideas, inventions, and charitable benefactions may have a substantial impact on the world. It's about daring to challenge traditions, disturb industriousness, and establish new routes of possibility.

Whether it's visioning a game-changing product or service, transubstantiating a mortal request, or addressing a significant social issue, featuring big requires the courage to suppose bravely and act aggressively in pursuit of one's vision.

Furthermore, dreaming large is not limited to business or entrepreneurship; it permeates all aspects of human activity. From scientific research to creative expression, social activism to personal development, great dreams fuel innovation, drive progress, and inspire good change across disciplines and industries. It is the force that drives individuals and societies to push beyond the known, to explore unknown territory, and to strive for perfection in the pursuit of their highest goals.

However, thinking large does not come without hurdles and impediments. The route to achieving ambitious goals is frequently plagued with uncertainty, struggle, and doubt. It necessitates resilience in the face of setbacks, tenacity in the face of adversity, and adaptation in the aftermath of unexpected problems. Furthermore, it necessitates a willingness to take risks, accept failure as a vital step toward success, and learn and grow from each experience along the way.

Despite the inherent challenges, the benefits of thinking large are immense. It is the satisfaction of knowing that one has dared to pursue one's passions and instincts, the thrill of witnessing one's vision come true, and the fulfillment of making a significant impact in the world. Furthermore, it is the legacy of inspiration and impact that one leaves for future generations, encouraging others to dream large and strive for the stars in their own life.

Dreaming big is not limited to a single moment of inspiration; it is an ongoing process of imagination, discovery, and development. It entails stretching the boundaries of what is familiar and comfortable, exploring unfamiliar ground, and accepting the inherent ambiguity and complexity of the trip ahead.

One of the most important components of dreaming big is the desire to question conventional thinking and go beyond the box. It encourages people to challenge current conventions and beliefs, to envisage possibilities that others may overlook, and to consider innovative approaches to problems and opportunities. Entrepreneurs may uncover new ideas and drive disruptive change in their industry by breaking free from conventional thinking limits.

Furthermore, dreaming big is inextricably linked with the concept of purpose and meaning. It is about connecting one's objectives to a greater sense of purpose and values, and seeking to make a positive difference in the world. Whether it's tackling social inequity, advancing environmental sustainability, or improving quality of life, dreaming big entails pursuing goals that are consistent with one's core views and ideals while also benefiting society.

Another essential component of dreaming big is the ability to endure in the face of adversity and uncertainty. Building a successful startup takes perseverance, courage, and resolve to overcome unavoidable obstacles and failures. It's about keeping your focus and momentum even when the way ahead appears difficult or unclear, and refusing to be discouraged by brief setbacks or impediments.

In essence, dreaming big is a transforming force that motivates individuals and organizations to go above their apparent boundaries and accomplish amazing results. It is about daring to envisage a future beyond the realm of possibility and taking brave action to make that vision a reality. Entrepreneurs that embrace the power of imagination, purpose, tenacity, and invention can open up new horizons of potential and leave a lasting impact on the world.

CHAPTER 2: LAYING THE FOUNDATION

Laying the Foundation is a critical stage in the path of any startup, comparable to laying the cornerstone of a building. It is the stage at which entrepreneurs transform their unique ideas into practical realities by building the foundational elements required for success. This phase entails a variety of responsibilities, including developing the business idea, establishing the organizational structure, and obtaining first funding.

Define the Vision: At the heart of laying the groundwork is the vision that will propel the startup forward. Entrepreneurs must create a clear and appealing vision for their venture, including its purpose, goals, and values. This vision serves as a guiding light, influencing strategic decisions and uniting stakeholders around a common goal.

Market Research and Analysis: Before jumping into execution, extensive market research is required. Entrepreneurs must thoroughly grasp their target market, including client demands, preferences, and pain points. Market study allows them to find opportunities, evaluate competitors, and fine-tune their value proposition in order to gain a distinct competitive advantage.

Company Planning: Creating a detailed company strategy is critical for charting a way forward. This includes defining the business model, revenue sources, marketing strategy, operational plan, and financial predictions. A well-structured business plan not only acts as a road map, but it also gives a framework for assessing progress and making strategic changes as needed.

Cultivating Partnerships and Networks: Establishing strategic alliances and networks inside the sector can bring essential resources, opportunities, and support. Entrepreneurs should aggressively engage with stakeholders, such as suppliers, distributors, mentors, and industry groups, to use their knowledge, insights, and connections. Collaborative alliances can help to speed growth, open up new markets, and reduce the risks involved with corporate expansion.

In essence, building the groundwork establishes the framework for the startup's path from inception to success. Entrepreneurs can lay a solid foundation for their startup to thrive and become a star in the competitive landscape by focusing on defining the vision, conducting extensive market research, crafting a robust business plan, ensuring legal compliance, building a talented team, securing funding, establishing infrastructure, and cultivating partnerships.

Embracing Agility and Flexibility: While a well-defined strategy is essential, startups must also embrace agility and flexibility during the foundation-laying phase. The corporate environment is dynamic, and unexpected difficulties or opportunities may occur. Entrepreneurs must be willing to pivot, iterate, and adjust their strategy depending on changing market trends, customer feedback, and internal learnings. Maintaining an agile attitude enables entrepreneurs to better overcome uncertainty and capitalize on new opportunities.

Fostering an Innovation Culture: Innovation is at the heart of startups, driving differentiation and competitive advantage. During the foundation-laying phase, entrepreneurs should foster an innovative culture within their firm. This includes encouraging team members to be creative, experiment, and learn on a regular basis. Startups may build an innovative culture that fuels growth and fosters resilience in the face of obstacles by creating an atmosphere in which new ideas are encouraged and failure is recognized as a learning opportunity.

Prioritizing Customer Centricity: Placing the customer at the center of everything is critical to startup success. During the foundation-laying phase, entrepreneurs should focus on understanding and addressing client wants, preferences, and pain points. This includes obtaining feedback from surveys, interviews, and usability testing and applying the results to improve product offerings, improve user experience, and establish long-term relationships with customers. Startups can build a loyal client base and achieve long-term success by providing value and solving real-world problems for their target market.

Managing hazards and Uncertainty: Startups operate in a dynamic and uncertain world, with hazards lurking at every corner. During the foundation-laying phase, entrepreneurs must efficiently identify, assess, and manage risks in order to ensure their venture's success. This includes conducting risk assessments, creating contingency plans, and adopting risk management measures to reduce potential company hazards. Startups may boost their resilience and ability to weather problems while capitalizing on opportunities by managing risks and uncertainty proactively.

Embracing Diversity and Inclusion: Startups benefit from both ethical imperatives and strategic advantages. During the foundation-laying phase, entrepreneurs should prioritize the formation of diverse and inclusive teams comprised of people from various backgrounds, opinions, and experiences. Embracing diversity promotes creativity, innovation, and adaptation, allowing entrepreneurs to better comprehend and service a varied client base while outperforming competition in the long run.

Measuring and Monitoring Progress: Defining key performance indicators (KPIs) and metrics is critical for tracking progress and performance during the foundation-laying stage. Entrepreneurs should set quantifiable goals and milestones that are consistent with their overall vision and business objectives. Startups that frequently monitor and analyze data can acquire significant insights into their strengths, shortcomings, and areas for progress, allowing them to make educated decisions and course adjustments as needed to stay on track for success.

Staying Resilient and Persistent: Starting a business is a difficult and often turbulent path that requires resilience and persistence. During the foundation-laying phase, entrepreneurs are likely to face setbacks, failures, and challenges. It is critical to create a resilient mindset.

Maintain unflinching determination in the face of hardship. Startups can overcome barriers and emerge stronger on the way to success by viewing failures as learning opportunities, remaining focused on long-term goals, and persevering through challenges.

CHAPTER 3: NAVIGATING CHALLENGES

Navigating challenges is an unavoidable element of the entrepreneurial journey, as entrepreneurs face a plethora of roadblocks and setbacks on their way to success. Whether it's request volatility, budget limits, or internal disagreements, how entrepreneurs deal with these problems can often decide the outcome of their venture.

To overcome hurdles and emerge stronger on the other side, you must be adaptable, rigid, and strategic in your approach. Related Challenges The first step in overcoming problems is to recognize and accept their existence. Entrepreneurs must maintain an acute awareness of potential implicit impediments, both internal and external. This includes undertaking extensive threat assessments, obtaining feedback from stakeholders, and remaining responsive to changes in the business landscape. Startups may proactively anticipate obstacles and build contingency plans and mitigation techniques to handle them before they become serious issues. Prioritizing Challenges Entrepreneurs must prioritize difficulties based on their influence on the business. Some hurdles, such as financial inflow issues or product recalls, may have an immediate impact on the adventure's viability, but others, such as request achromatism or nonsupervisory adjustments, may have a longer-term impact. By prioritizing difficulties and allocating funds accordingly, businesses may focus their efforts on addressing the most pressing concerns while minimizing their negative implications. Building Resilience. Resilience is the ability to recover from setbacks and persevere in the face of adversity. Startups must establish a culture of adaptation within their organization, instilling a sense of optimism, tenacity, and perseverance among unit members. This includes providing emotional support, recognizing modest victories, and learning from setbacks in order to develop adaptability and fiber in the face of future challenges. Entrepreneurs should also use tone-care and stress-management techniques in order to retain their personal adaptability and well-being during difficult times. Seeking Support: No entrepreneur can face obstacles alone, and getting help from instructors, counsellors, and peers can provide invaluable guidance and perspective. Establishing a robust support network allows entrepreneurs to draw into the collaborative expertise and experience of people who have faced and overcome similar issues. This could include joining networking groups, attending assiduity events, or seeking formal mentorship relationships to receive insight and advise from experienced professionals. Embracing rigidity In the midst of uncertainty and change, entrepreneurs must embrace rigidity as a guiding principle. This entails being willing to pivot and reaffirm their business model, strategy, or product immolation in response to shifting demand dynamics or customer feedback. Entrepreneurs that remain adaptable and open-minded can seize new opportunities, avoid mistakes, and stay ahead of the competition in an ever-changing business landscape. Learning From Failure Failure is an unavoidable aspect of the business journey, but it is also a valuable literacy opportunity. Rather than perceiving failure as a setback, entrepreneurs should see it as an opportunity to learn, grow, and improve. Startups can turn failures into stepping stones to future success by performing posthumous studies of failed enterprises, identifying fundamental causes of failure, and rooting out valuable lessons gained.

Staying Agile: Agility is critical for startups to manage problems successfully because it allows them to respond swiftly and decisively to changing conditions. This includes implementing agile approaches and processes that emphasize iterative development, quick experimentation, and continuous improvement. By breaking down projects into smaller, more manageable tasks and iterating on them based on feedback and results, entrepreneurs may quickly adapt to changing challenges and exploit new possibilities.

Entrepreneurs also face issues with market validation and client acquisition. Validating product-market fit is an important milestone for companies since it demonstrates demand for their goods and guides strategic decisions about product development and marketing. This process entails performing market research, collecting client input, and iterating on product features to meet market needs and preferences. Furthermore, to acquire clients in a crowded and competitive environment, businesses must develop successful marketing and sales strategies, raise brand awareness, and cultivate meaningful relationships with their target audiences. It is a continuous process of experimentation, optimization, and iteration to determine the most successful channels and messaging for reaching and engaging customers. Furthermore, startups frequently experience scalability issues. As demand for their products or services increases, entrepreneurs must expand their operations, infrastructure, and personnel to meet the demand while maintaining quality standards. Scaling successfully necessitates meticulous planning, investment in scalable technology and systems, and smart growth into new markets or consumer groups. Furthermore, entrepreneurs must traverse the intricacies of scaling without sacrificing agility, creativity, or culture, as rapid growth can strain resources and cause operational issues if not managed efficiently.

Companies may face problems connected to partnerships and

cooperation. Strategic collaboration with other enterprises, organizations, or stakeholders can give essential resources, opportunities, and support. However, negotiating the complexity of partnership agreements, setting mutually beneficial conditions, and sustaining productive relationships necessitates excellent communication, trust-building, and interest alignment.

Entrepreneurs must also be careful to protect their interests and intellectual property when entering into partnerships, ensuring that

agreements are fair, equitable, and enforceable.

Furthermore, startups confront issues in achieving a healthy work-life balance and controlling stress and burnout. Entrepreneurship may be all-consuming, with long hours, huge levels of responsibility, and constant pressure to perform. Finding the right balance between work, personal life, and self-care is critical for long-term success and well-being. Entrepreneurs must emphasize self-care, set boundaries, and seek support from friends, family, and mentors to avoid burnout and remain resilient in the face of hardship.

CHAPTER 4: THE ART OF LEADERSHIP

The art of leadership is more than just management; it is about inspiring, empowering, and directing others to reach their full potential and collaborate toward a common vision. In the context of startups and entrepreneurship, good leadership is critical for encouraging innovation, generating growth, and navigating the complexity of the business environment.

At its foundation, leadership is creating a compelling vision and direction for the business, defining specific goals and objectives, and persuading people to support that vision. It is about creating an aspirational and achievable vision of the future, as well as fostering a feeling of purpose and meaning in people's work. Effective leaders communicate their vision with clarity, passion, and honesty, fostering a sense of alignment and unity among teammates.

Leadership entails establishing and maintaining good relationships founded on trust, respect, and empathy. Leaders must foster an environment of openness, transparency, and inclusivity in which people feel appreciated, heard, and empowered to share their unique viewpoints and skills. Leaders may build a sense of belonging and camaraderie, resulting in a supportive and collaborative workplace that encourages teamwork and innovation. Effective leadership entails encouraging and equipping others to take ownership and initiative in the pursuit of organizational goals. It is about recognizing and developing team members' potential by giving mentorship, coaching, and support to help them grow and flourish. Leaders empower individuals by delegating authority, supporting autonomy, and cultivating an accountability culture.

Additionally, leadership entails setting an example and exhibiting integrity, resiliency, and ethical behavior in all facets of the firm. Leaders must maintain high levels of honesty, fairness, and integrity while holding themselves and others accountable for their activities. Leaders develop trust and credibility by exhibiting the values and behaviors they expect others to exhibit, as well as inspiring loyalty and commitment among team members.

Furthermore, effective leadership necessitates flexibility and agility in the face of change and uncertainty. Leaders must be able to negotiate complexity, uncertainty, and volatility while pivoting swiftly in response to changing market dynamics and new problems. Leaders who are aware of external trends and internal dynamics may foresee change, grab opportunities, and position their businesses for success in an ever-changing.

The art of leadership is more than just management; it is about inspiring, empowering, and directing others to reach their full potential and collaborate toward a common vision. In the context of startups and entrepreneurship, good leadership is critical for encouraging innovation, generating growth, and navigating the complexity of the business environment.

At its foundation, leadership is creating a compelling vision and direction for the business, defining specific goals and objectives, and persuading people to support that vision. It is about creating an aspirational and achievable vision of the future, as well as fostering a feeling of purpose and meaning in people's work. Effective leaders communicate their vision with clarity, passion, and honesty, fostering a sense of alignment and unity among teammates.

Leadership entails establishing and maintaining good relationships founded on trust, respect, and empathy. Leaders must foster an environment of openness, transparency, and inclusivity in which people feel appreciated, heard, and empowered to share their unique viewpoints and skills. Leaders may build a sense of belonging and camaraderie, resulting in a supportive and collaborative workplace that encourages teamwork and innovation. Effective leadership entails encouraging and equipping others to take ownership and initiative in the pursuit of organizational goals. It is about recognizing and developing team members' potential by giving mentorship, coaching, and support to help them grow and flourish. Leaders empower individuals by delegating authority, supporting autonomy, and cultivating an accountability culture.

Additionally, leadership entails setting an example and exhibiting integrity, resiliency, and ethical behavior in all facets of the firm. Leaders must maintain high levels of honesty, fairness, and integrity while holding themselves and others accountable for their activities. Leaders develop trust and credibility by exhibiting the values and behaviors they expect others to exhibit, as well as inspiring loyalty and commitment among team members.

Furthermore, effective leadership necessitates flexibility and agility in the face of change and uncertainty. Leaders must be able to negotiate complexity, uncertainty, and volatility while pivoting swiftly in response to changing market dynamics and new problems. Leaders who are aware of external trends and internal dynamics may foresee change, grab opportunities, and position their businesses for success in an ever-changing.

CHAPTER 5: INNOVATION AND ADAPTATION

In the dynamic geography of entrepreneurship, innovation and adaptation are the two pillars that drive success. In a world marked by quick technological improvements, shifting consumer preferences, and evolving request dynamics, startups must be ready to introduce and adapt in order to remain competitive, applicable, and flexible in the face of question and disruption. At its core, invention entails the development and implementation of new ideas, outcomes, or processes to address unmet needs, solve complicated issues, or capitalize on emerging opportunities. It is about questioning the current quo, allowing for creativity, and pushing the limits of what is possible. In the startup context, creativity extends beyond product development to include all parts of the firm, from marketing and negotiations to operations and customer experience. A culture that encourages creativity, experimentation, and risk-taking is an important driver of innovation in startups.

Leaders have an important role in establishing such a culture by fostering open communication, valuing diversity of studies, and rewarding action and imagination. Startups may unleash the full potential of its platoon members and promote ceaseless creativity by fostering an environment in where ideas are valued, failure is considered as a learning opportunity, and cooperation is encouraged. Furthermore, companies must be agile and adaptive in response to changing request conditions, client feedback, and competition challenges. Adaptation entails detecting and responding quickly to changes in the external terrain, seizing new opportunities, and mitigating risks. To keep ahead of the competition and capitalize on emerging trends, it is necessary to be able to pivot strategy, reinforce products or services, and reallocate funds as needed. Similarly, entrepreneurs can promote innovation through strategic partnerships, collaborations, and ecosystems. Startups can speed up innovation, gain access to new requests, and overcome resource constraints by leveraging external stakeholders' moxie, coffers, and networks. Startups can leverage a multitude of expertise and capacities to drive development and isolation, whether through co-creation with guests, strategic collaborations with assiduity partners, or involvement in invention capitals and accelerators. Furthermore, invention in startups usually entails the use of technology to disrupt existing business models and create new value propositions. Whether through the development of personal software, the abandonment of emerging technologies such as artificial intelligence or blockchain, or the integration of digital tools and platforms, startups can use technology to streamline processes, improve client experiences, and unleash new revenue streams.

Startups must adopt a philosophy of continual improvement and iteration in their pursuit of innovation. Startups can optimize their services and drive incremental innovation over time by asking customer input, iterating on product prototypes, and performing hypothesis-testing tests. It is a continuous process of learning, adaptation, and refining that allows entrepreneurs to stay ahead of the competition and provide value to their customers in an ever-changing environment.

Innovation and adaptation are continuous processes that demand dedication, perseverance, and a willingness to embrace change. Startups must constantly monitor the horizon for emerging trends, technology, and opportunities, and be proactive in responding to changing market dynamics. This requires being alert to client input, watching rival activities, and receiving insights from industry experts and thought leaders.

Furthermore, creativity in startups frequently requires the development of a growth mentality among team members. A growth mindset is defined as a conviction in one's ability to learn, adapt, and improve over time. Leaders may encourage a growth mindset by encouraging skill development, praising progress and accomplishments, and viewing setbacks as chances for learning and growth. Startups may encourage their team members to accept challenges, take risks, and endure in the face of adversity, allowing them to reach their full potential and drive internal innovation.

Entrepreneurs can stimulate innovation by implementing agile approaches and practices. Agile principles prioritize flexibility, cooperation, and iterative development, enabling businesses to respond swiftly to changing requirements and feedback. Startups may speed innovation and produce goods and services that match their customers' changing demands by breaking down projects into smaller, more manageable chunks, prioritizing customer value, and regularly testing and iterating on solutions.

Additionally, startups can foster innovation by emphasizing user-centric design and human-centered innovation. Startups may create products and services that engage strongly with their target audience by prioritizing their consumers' needs, preferences, and experiences during the design phase. This includes performing user research, creating solutions, and collecting feedback via user testing and iteration. Startups may develop delightful and loyal goods and experiences by empathizing with their people and designing with their needs in mind.

CHAPTER 6: MARKETING MASTERY

Marketing mastery is the practice of effectively advertising products, services, or brands to specific audiences in order to increase awareness, engagement, and sales. In the context of startups and entrepreneurship, mastering marketing is critical for establishing brand awareness, attracting customers, and driving sustainable growth in a competitive market.

Marketing mastery is fundamentally about knowing target customers' needs, preferences, and habits and personalizing marketing plans and methods to them. This necessitates extensive market research, segmentation, and analysis to uncover crucial demographics, psychographics, and purchasing behaviors. By understanding their target audience's desires, pain areas, and motivations, entrepreneurs can create compelling value propositions and marketing that successfully express the unique benefits of their offerings.

Furthermore, marketing competence includes a wide range of channels and methods, both online and offline, that businesses can use to reach and engage their intended audience. This encompasses traditional channels like print advertising, direct mail, and event marketing, as well as digital channels like social media, search engine optimization (SEO), content marketing, email marketing, and influencer collaborations. Startups can increase their reach and influence across several touchpoints in the customer journey by taking a multi-channel approach and integrating various methods into a unified marketing plan.

Furthermore, marketing expertise entails creating captivating stories and branding that connects with target consumers emotionally. Effective branding extends beyond logos and colors to include a brand's overall perception and personality, such as its values, voice, and visual identity. By building a strong brand narrative and consistent brand messaging, companies may create a memorable and unified brand experience that resonates with customers and develops brand loyalty over time.

Furthermore, marketing expertise necessitates a data-driven approach to measurement, analysis, and optimization. Startups must monitor key performance indicators (KPIs) such as website traffic, conversion rates, client acquisition expenses, and return on investment (ROI) to assess the efficiency of their marketing campaigns. Startups can use analytics tools and data insights to spot patterns, discover opportunities, and optimize marketing strategies for maximum effect and efficiency.

Furthermore, marketing expertise requires being adaptable and responsive to shifting market trends, consumer preferences, and competitive landscapes. Startups must constantly monitor the competitive landscape, study industry trends, and solicit client feedback in order to tailor their marketing strategy and methods. Experimenting with new channels, iterating on messaging, or modifying targeting criteria can help you stay ahead of the curve and capitalize on emerging opportunities.

Furthermore, marketing mastery goes beyond client acquisition to include customer retention and loyalty. Repeat customers are often more valuable than new ones since they spend more, refer others, and help to ensure the long-term viability of the business. Startups can cultivate customer connections through personalized communication, loyalty programs, and great customer service, instilling trust, contentment, and loyalty in customers, keeping them coming back for more.

Marketing mastery also entails leveraging the power of content marketing to educate, engage, and inspire target audiences. material marketing is the process of developing and distributing interesting, relevant, and high-quality material, such as blog posts, articles, videos, infographics, and podcasts, that resonates with target audiences and leads to significant interactions and conversions. Startups can portray themselves as trusted industry experts by delivering important insights, information, and entertainment, gradually building credibility and trust with their audience.

Furthermore, marketing expertise includes the strategic use of social media to increase brand visibility, encourage community participation, and drive conversions. Social media networks like Facebook, Instagram, Twitter, LinkedIn, and TikTok provide effective tools for reaching and communicating with target audiences in real time. Startups can use social media to distribute information, communicate with followers, execute targeted advertising campaigns, and track conversations and trends in order to remain relevant and responsive to customer requirements and preferences.

Furthermore, marketing expertise entails using effective pricing and packaging methods to increase value and profitability. Startups must carefully evaluate pricing methods such as cost-plus pricing, value-based pricing, or competitive pricing, as well as establish the best pricing tiers, bundles, and promotions to attract customers and increase sales. Startups can maximize revenue and profitability by aligning price with perceived value and consumer expectations.

Furthermore, marketing mastery necessitates a thorough awareness of the customer experience and the optimization of touchpoints to increase conversions and retention. Startups must map the whole customer experience, from awareness to purchase to advocacy, and identify key touchpoints where they may impact consumer behavior and drive desired behaviors. Startups may decrease friction, boost engagement, and drive more conversions and sales by optimizing their website design, user experience, and conversion funnels.

Furthermore, marketing expertise entails forming strategic alliances and collaborations to broaden reach, enter new markets, and accelerate mutual progress. Partnerships with similar businesses, influencers, or industry groups can offer startups with access to new audiences, resources, and knowledge that they would not otherwise have. Startups can boost their marketing efforts, increase their credibility, and open up new chances for development and expansion by forming mutually beneficial relationships.

CHAPTER 7: SCALING HEIGHTS

Scaling heights is the ambitious path of growth and expansion that enterprises take to reach new heights of achievement, impact, and influence. Scaling heights in the context of startups and entrepreneurship means pursuing ambitious goals, overcoming barriers, and realizing one's full potential in the pursuit of greatness.

At its essence, scaling heights entails transcending the constraints of the existing quo and pushing for new vistas of opportunity. It is about going beyond one's comfort zone, accepting challenges, and seizing opportunities to propel oneself and one's company to new heights of success. Scaling heights, whether it's entering new markets, releasing breakthrough products, or exceeding sales targets, necessitates vision, determination, and an unwavering pursuit of perfection.

Strategic planning and execution are important factors in reaching new heights. Startups must create a clear growth plan that includes defined goals, milestones, and tactics for reaching them. This may include conducting market research, identifying untapped prospects, and creating executable expansion plans. Startups can map a road for success by defining ambitious but attainable goals and executing them with precision and dedication.

Reaching new heights necessitates a commitment to ongoing innovation and progress. Startups must constantly innovate and iterate on their products, services, and processes in order to be competitive in the marketplace. This entails cultivating a culture of innovation, experimentation, and learning within the business, as well as allowing team members to question norms, take chances, and push the boundaries of what is possible. Startups can accelerate their success by adopting an innovative and adaptable mindset.

Scaling heights frequently entails entering new markets or consumer groups in order to provide new sources of growth and revenue. This may necessitate companies tailoring their goods to fit the requirements and tastes of other audiences, localizing their marketing and sales activities, and navigating regulatory and cultural variations in international regions. Startups can reduce risks and seize possibilities for long-term growth and expansion by diversifying their client base and global presence.

Furthermore, increasing heights necessitates a focus on developing scalable infrastructure and processes that allow development without sacrificing efficiency or quality. Startups must invest in technology, infrastructure, and talent that can grow with the company and handle increased demand and complexity. To enhance efficiency and reduce bottlenecks, repetitive processes may be automated, workflows streamlined, and resource allocation optimized. Startups that lay a solid basis for growth can scale more successfully and sustainably over time.

Furthermore, scaling heights entails forming strategic collaborations and alliances to broaden reach, gain access to new resources, and accelerate mutual progress. Whether through collaborations with industry peers, strategic alliances with complementary businesses, or partnerships with key stakeholders, entrepreneurs can harness their partners' total experience, networks, and resources to accelerate growth and make a bigger impact. Startups can attain heights that would be difficult or impossible for them to achieve on their own by forming strong and mutually beneficial relationships.

Scaling heights also necessitates the development of strong leadership and organizational capabilities to negotiate the difficulties of expansion and change. As businesses grow and evolve, they must have a leadership team capable of inspiring, motivating, and aligning people around a common vision and plan. This includes building leadership qualities such as strategic thinking, communication, decision-making, and emotional intelligence, as well as enabling leaders at all levels of the business to drive results and foster an accountable and high performance culture.

Furthermore, scaling heights necessitates a focus on customer success and satisfaction in order to increase retention, loyalty, and advocacy. As startups develop, they must prioritize providing excellent customer experiences and exceeding consumer expectations at all touchpoints. This includes listening to customer feedback, fixing problem spots, and anticipating and meeting consumer demands. Startups can nurture a loyal client base by developing strong customer relationships and providing value beyond the transaction, which promotes long-term growth and success.

Furthermore, scaling heights frequently entails raising funds to fund expansion activities and drive growth. Depending on their stage of growth and financial demands, startups might seek funding from a variety of sources, including venture capital, angel investment, crowdsourcing, or debt finance. To secure investment, companies must explain a compelling value proposition, demonstrate traction and scalability, and cultivate trusting, transparent, and mutually beneficial relationships with investors. Startups can expedite their journey to reaching heights and achieving their ambitious goals by gaining access to the funding they require to carry out their expansion plans.

Reaching new heights necessitates a dedication to operational excellence and efficiency in order to maximize resources and increase profitability. Startups must constantly assess and improve their business processes, systems, and workflows in order to minimize waste, cut costs, and boost productivity. This could include using lean concepts, using agile approaches, and leveraging technology and automation to streamline operations and increase productivity. Startups that operate more effectively can better deploy resources, reinvesting savings in growth projects and innovation to catapult themselves to new heights of success.

Scaling heights requires adequate risk management to ensure the business's long-term survival and sustainability. As a startup grows, it may face additional obstacles and uncertainties, such as market volatility, regulatory changes, or competition threats.

Startups must do rigorous risk assessments, create contingency plans, and implement robust risk management systems to limit potential threats and defend against negative consequences. By proactively identifying and mitigating risks, entrepreneurs can better overcome hurdles and remain resilient in the face of adversity on their path to success.

CHAPTER 8: FINANCIAL FITNESS

Financial fitness is a condition of financial well-being and stability attained via good financial management, disciplined saving and spending habits, and prudent investment selections. Financial health is critical in the context of startups and entrepreneurship to ensure the company's long-term viability, growth, and success.

At its core, financial fitness is laying a sound financial foundation based on a thorough understanding of the company's financial condition, cash flow, and financial objectives. Startups must create thorough financial plans and budgets that detail revenue projections, spending forecasts, and capital requirements for a specific time period. Startups may make educated decisions and utilize resources more efficiently to support their growth objectives by setting clear financial targets and tracking progress toward them.

Furthermore, financial health necessitates careful cash flow management to provide sufficient liquidity and solvency to satisfy short-term obligations and support continuous operations. Startups must carefully monitor cash inflows and outflows, efficiently manage working capital, and anticipate and plan for cash flow volatility. This could include using cash flow forecasting tools, arranging favorable payment terms with suppliers, and keeping a cash reserve to handle unforeseen needs or crises.

Furthermore, financial fitness includes strategic debt management to maximize leverage while minimizing financial risk. Startups may use debt financing to raise funds for expansion projects, but they must do it wisely and responsibly to prevent overleveraging and high debt burdens. This includes determining the cost of debt, reviewing repayment conditions, and ensuring that debt obligations are sustainable and in line with the company's cash flow and revenue generation capacities.

Furthermore, financial fitness entails increasing revenue creation and profitability through smart pricing strategies, revenue optimization, and cost-cutting initiatives. Startups must discover and capitalize on revenue possibilities, optimize pricing models, and implement cost-cutting initiatives in order to increase margins and profitability. This may include conducting pricing assessments, identifying areas of inefficiency or waste, and putting in place steps to simplify processes and minimize overhead costs.

Furthermore, financial fitness necessitates smart investment and capital allocation to drive growth and innovation while maximising returns for stakeholders. Startups must carefully examine investment opportunities, weigh potential risks and returns, and prioritize investments that are consistent with the company's strategic goals and long-term vision. This could include investing in R&D, technological infrastructure, talent acquisition, or market growth activities that have the potential to provide considerable value and competitive advantage over time.

Furthermore, financial fitness requires establishing and maintaining effective financial controls and governance systems to protect assets, prevent fraud and misbehavior, and assure regulatory compliance. Startups must build strong financial reporting systems, internal controls, and audit processes in order to track financial performance, uncover anomalies or irregularities, and ensure transparency and accountability.

Financial fitness entails cultivating and maintaining positive connections with important stakeholders like as investors, lenders, suppliers, and customers. Startups must communicate openly and proactively with their stakeholders, offering regular updates on financial performance, strategic initiatives, and risk factors that may affect their interests. Building trust and credibility with stakeholders allows businesses to gain easier access to funding, negotiate better terms, and use relationships to assist their growth and expansion efforts.

Furthermore, financial health necessitates a dedication to lifelong learning and education in order to keep up with changing financial trends, legislation, and best practices. Startups must invest in continual training and development for finance and accounting professionals, as well as senior leadership and board members, to ensure that they have the knowledge and skills required to make sound judgments and efficiently handle complicated financial difficulties. This could include attending seminars, workshops, or industry conferences, as well as obtaining professional certifications or higher degrees in finance or accounting.

Furthermore, financial fitness includes strategic tax planning and compliance to maximize tax efficiency and reduce tax liabilities. Startups must keep up with changes in tax laws and regulations, discover possibilities for tax savings, and create tax strategies that are aligned with their business goals and objectives. This could include structuring business transactions and investments in a tax-efficient manner, taking advantage of available tax credits and deductions, and working with tax experts or consultants to guarantee compliance with applicable tax rules and regulations.

Additionally, financial fitness entails diversifying revenue streams and income sources in order to lessen dependency on a single source of money and mitigate risk. Startups should look into ways to expand their product or service offerings, target new consumer segments or markets, or create alternative revenue streams like licensing, franchising, or subscription-based models. Startups can boost their resistance to economic downturns, market changes, and other external shocks that may affect their major sources of revenue by diversifying their revenue streams.

Furthermore, financial fitness necessitates proactive risk management and contingency planning to account for unforeseen occurrences or disruptions that could jeopardize financial stability. Startups must identify potential business risks, such as supply chain interruptions, cybersecurity attacks, and natural calamities, and devise mitigation techniques to reduce their impact. This may include obtaining insurance, setting up emergency funds, or creating business continuity plans to ensure that operations can continue uninterrupted in the case of a disaster.

CHAPTER 9: CULTIVATING SUCCESS

Cultivating success is the deliberate and planned process of creating the conditions, behaviors, and mindsets that lead to success, fulfillment, and wealth. In the context of startups and entrepreneurship, nurturing success entails building an atmosphere that encourages creativity, growth, and resilience, as well as empowering individuals to reach their full potential and contribute meaningfully to the organization's mission and goals.

One of the most important aspects of developing success is creating an organizational culture of excellence and continual development. Setting high standards for performance, quality, and innovation, as well as providing the necessary support, resources, and incentives, helps individuals and teams achieve their full potential. Startups can foster a culture of success by cultivating a growth mentality, encouraging experimentation and learning, and celebrating accomplishments and milestones.

Furthermore, cultivating success necessitates effective leadership and mentorship to guide, inspire, and assist individuals as they navigate their professional and personal lives.

Leaders have an important role in establishing the tone and direction for the business, modeling the values and behaviors that lead to success, and enabling people to take ownership and initiative in achieving common goals. Leaders can foster a culture of trust, collaboration, and responsibility in their teams by acting as role models, coaches, and advocates. This culture supports success and promotes organizational performance. Furthermore, cultivating success requires developing resilience and adaptability in the face of obstacles and setbacks. Startups are inherently risky endeavors, and setbacks are unavoidable on the road to success. Cultivating a resilient mindset entails viewing mistakes as chances for growth and learning, accepting change and uncertainty as natural components of the entrepreneurial path, and having a positive attitude and a sense of tenacity in the face of setbacks. Startups that cultivate resilience and adaptability can weather the inevitable storms and emerge stronger and more resilient on the other side.

Furthermore, cultivating success requires promoting diversity, equity, and inclusion inside the business in order to maximize the potential of all individuals and develop a culture of belonging and empowerment. Startups must aggressively encourage diversity and inclusion in their hiring, promotion, and leadership development strategies, as well as foster an environment in which people of all backgrounds feel appreciated, respected, and supported. Startups that embrace varied viewpoints, experiences, and ideas may inspire creativity, innovation, and resilience, as well as build a more inclusive and equitable workplace where everyone can grow and succeed.

Furthermore, building success entails developing a customer-centric mindset and maintaining a relentless emphasis on delivering value and impact. Startups must emphasize knowing their consumers' requirements, preferences, and aspirations, and then create goods, services, and experiences that exceed their expectations and solve their most pressing problems. Startups that prioritize the client in everything they do can cultivate committed advocates and ambassadors who drive growth, profitability, and long-term success.

Cultivating success entails creating an organizational culture of openness, trust, and open communication. Startups must foster an environment in which team members feel comfortable sharing ideas, opinions, and concerns, while also encouraging constructive debate and collaboration. Startups that promote transparency and open communication can break down barriers, create cooperation across teams and departments, and leverage their workforce's collective intelligence and creativity to drive innovation and problem-solving.

Furthermore, achieving success necessitates a dedication to ethical behavior and social responsibility in all parts of business operations.

Startups must act with integrity, honesty, and responsibility, and maintain high ethical standards in their relationships with consumers, employees, suppliers, and other stakeholders. Startups that prioritize ethical behavior and corporate social responsibility can build trust and credibility with stakeholders, differentiate themselves from competitors, and have a good effect in the communities they serve.

Furthermore, cultivating success entails creating an organizational culture of entrepreneurship and intrapreneurship in which employees are empowered to take the initiative, pursue new ideas, and drive good change. Startups must provide opportunity for employees to pursue their passions, learn new skills, and experiment with novel approaches to business difficulties. Startups may promote development and innovation from within by instilling an entrepreneurial mindset in their employees and offering resources and support for intrapreneurial initiatives.

Furthermore, achieving success necessitates a dedication to sustainability and environmental stewardship in corporate practices and operations. Startups must evaluate the environmental impact of their products, services, and supply chains, and take proactive measures to reduce their carbon footprint, waste, and natural resource consumption. Startups that implement sustainable business practices can demonstrate their commitment to corporate responsibility, attract environmentally concerned customers and investors, and help to create a more sustainable and resilient future for all.

Furthermore, creating success entails fostering a culture of learning and resilience, in which individuals are encouraged to view failure as an opportunity for growth and development. Startups must foster an environment that encourages experimentation and empowers individuals to take chances, learn from mistakes, and adapt in the face of adversity. By establishing a culture of continuous learning and resilience, startups can build a staff that is agile, adaptive, and equipped to flourish in an ever-changing business landscape. Cultivating success is a complicated process that necessitates a comprehensive approach to leadership, culture, ethics, sustainability, and learning. Startups can create an environment in which individuals can thrive and the organization can achieve its goals and have a positive impact on the world by fostering transparency, trust, and open communication, prioritizing ethical behavior and corporate social responsibility, nurturing entrepreneurship and intrapreneurship, embracing sustainability and environmental stewardship, and promoting a culture of learning and resilience.

CHAPTER 10: MAKING AN IMPACT

Making an impact entails causing substantial and long-term change in the world around us by our activities, projects, and contributions. It is about using our abilities, resources, and influence to address critical issues, empower others, and achieve great results for individuals, communities, and society as a whole. In the context of startups and entrepreneurship, making an impact extends beyond financial success to include social, environmental, and cultural factors that contribute to a better society.

One of the key aspects of making an impact involves recognizing and addressing unmet needs and societal concerns through innovative solutions and efforts. Startups offer a unique chance to address urgent issues such as poverty, inequality, climate change, healthcare access, education, and sustainability by creating innovative products, services, and business models. Startups that focus on purpose-driven innovation and social entrepreneurship can produce value not only for their shareholders, but also for society as a whole.

Making an impact entails incorporating social responsibility and ethical business practices into all parts of operations and decision-making. Startups must evaluate the social, environmental, and ethical consequences of their actions and seek to act with integrity, openness, and responsibility. This may include implementing sustainable corporate practices, fostering diversity and inclusion, assisting local communities, and maintaining high ethical standards in relationships with stakeholders. Startups that prioritize social responsibility can generate trust, credibility, and goodwill with customers, workers, investors, and the broader society, resulting in a beneficial impact that goes far beyond their bottom line. Making an impact necessitates a dedication to promoting diversity, equity, and inclusion within the firm and the larger ecosystem. Startups must provide opportunity for people from different backgrounds and underrepresented groups to participate and flourish in entrepreneurship, innovation, and leadership. Startups that embrace diversity of ideas, experiences, and viewpoints may fuel creativity, innovation, and resilience, as well as create a more inclusive and fair society in which everyone has the opportunity to flourish and prosper.

making an impact entails empowering and inspiring others to attain their full potential and contribute to constructive change. Startups can promote social and economic empowerment by offering mentorship programs, skill training, capital access, and assistance to small businesses and entrepreneurs in underrepresented communities. Startups that invest in human capital and build capacity at the grassroots level can establish pathways for individuals and communities facing structural barriers and disparities to achieve upward mobility, economic prosperity, and social mobility.

Making an impact requires assessing and conveying the social and environmental consequences of company activities and efforts. Startups must use metrics and frameworks for assessing effect, such as the United Nations Sustainable Development Goals (SDGs), and monitor progress toward key performance indicators (KPIs) for social, environmental, and economic consequences. Startups may hold themselves responsible to stakeholders by transparently reporting on their effect and success, inspiring others to take action, and driving collective efforts to achieve shared goals for a more sustainable and equitable future.

Making an influence is a diverse and idealistic activity that necessitates deliberateness, teamwork, and leadership at all levels of society. Startups can make a significant difference in the world by identifying and addressing pressing challenges through innovative solutions, prioritizing social responsibility and ethical business practices, fostering diversity and inclusion, empowering others to succeed, and drive collective efforts toward achieving shared goals for a more sustainable and equitable future.

CONCLUSION

As we reach the conclusion of "From Startup to Stardom," it's clear that the journey from humble beginnings to extraordinary success is not merely a destination, but a transformative odyssey filled with challenges, triumphs, and invaluable lessons learned along the way.

Throughout this book, we've explored the essential elements of startup success, from laying the foundation and dreaming big to navigating challenges, mastering marketing, and scaling heights. We've delved into the art of leadership, innovation, and adaptation, and uncovered the secrets to financial fitness, cultivating success, and making an impact that extends far beyond the bottom line.

But beyond the practical strategies and tactics lies a deeper truth: that the path to stardom is as much about the journey as it is about the destination. It's about the passion, determination, and resilience to pursue your dreams against all odds. It's about the courage to take risks, the willingness to fail, and the tenacity to get back up and try again.

As you close the final pages of this book, I urge you to remember that your journey as an entrepreneur is just beginning. Armed with the knowledge, insights, and inspiration found within these pages, you have the power to chart your own course, defy expectations, and write your own success story.

So go forth with confidence, ambition, and a relentless pursuit of excellence. Embrace the challenges, celebrate the victories, and never lose sight of the impact you have the potential to make on the world. For in the end, it's not the accolades or the achievements that define your legacy, but the lives you touch, the dreams you inspire, and the mark you leave on the world as you journey from startup to stardom.

From startup to stardom

www.ingramcontent.com/pod-product-compliance
Lightning Source LLC
Chambersburg PA
CBHW050101230526
45470CB00004B/1626